United States Government Accountability Office

Report to the Ranking Member, Committee on the Budget, United States Senate

I0448377

July 2013

FEDERAL VEHICLE FLEETS

Adopting Leading Practices Could Improve Management

FEDERAL VEHICLE FLEETS

Adopting Leading Practices Could Improve Management

GAO Highlights

Highlights of GAO-13-659, a report to the Ranking Member, Committee on the Budget, U.S. Senate

Why GAO Did This Study

Federal agencies (excluding the U.S. Postal Service) spend about $3 billion annually to acquire, operate, and maintain about 450,000 civilian and non-tactical military vehicles. Agencies may lease or buy vehicles from GSA, which also issues requirements and guidance on fleet management. In recent years, Congress and the President have raised concerns about the size and cost of federal agencies' fleets. In 2011, the President directed agencies to determine their optimal fleet inventories and set targets for achieving these inventories by 2015 with the goal of a more cost-effective fleet.

GAO was asked to review agency efforts to reduce fleet costs. This report addresses (1) the extent to which selected federal agencies use leading practices to manage their fleets, including their sizes and costs, and (2) any challenges these agencies face in managing their fleets and strategies they use to address these challenges. GAO selected USDA, DHS, Interior, VA, Air Force, and the Army Corps for review based on factors such as fleet size, fleet composition, and changes in fleet size from 2005 to 2011. To identify leading practices, GAO interviewed recognized private sector and government fleet management experts and GSA officials.

What GAO Recommends

GAO recommends that the Administrator of GSA 1) develop and publish guidance for agencies on estimating indirect fleet costs and 2) request that agencies provide supporting documentation on their methods for determining their optimal fleet inventories. GSA agreed with the recommendations.

View GAO-13-659. For more information, contact Susan Fleming at (202) 512-2834 or flemings@gao.gov.

What GAO Found

GAO identified three leading practices for fleet management and found that selected federal agencies—the Departments of Agriculture (USDA), Homeland Security (DHS), the Interior (Interior), and Veterans Affairs (VA); the U.S. Air Force (Air Force); and the Army Corps of Engineers (Army Corps)—follow these practices to varying degrees. These practices are 1) maintaining a well-designed fleet-management information system (FMIS), 2) analyzing life-cycle costs to inform investment decisions, and 3) optimizing fleet size and composition. GAO identified these practices based on views provided by recognized fleet experts and determined that the practices align with legal requirements and General Services Administration (GSA) recommendations.

- None of the agencies GAO reviewed capture in their FMISs all of the data elements recommended by GSA. The types of data missing most frequently are data on fleet costs, including indirect costs, such as salaries of personnel with fleet-related duties. Also, some of these systems are not integrated with other key agency systems. As a result, fleet managers face challenges in performing analyses that can guide fleet decisions. All of these agencies are making efforts to improve their data and FMISs, but some lack an approach for estimating indirect fleet costs. GSA's guidance does not discuss how to estimate these costs.

- Most of the selected agencies are not fully analyzing life-cycle costs to make decisions about when to replace vehicles. In addition, although most of the selected agencies use life-cycle cost analyses to decide whether to lease or purchase vehicles, some agencies' analyses do not consider a full set of costs. As a result, agencies may not have full information with which to make vehicle replacement and procurement decisions. Officials mainly cited problems with their cost data and FMISs as contributing factors, and efforts to improve in these areas have the potential to enhance agencies' ability to conduct these types of analyses.

- In response to the President's 2011 directive and related GSA guidance, the selected agencies have set targets for achieving optimal fleet size and composition. Planned changes in fleet sizes from 2011 to 2015 range from DHS's 15 percent fleet reduction to VA's 8 percent increase. GSA reviewed agencies' initial targets in 2012 and recommended some changes, but lacked supporting documentation to explain how most agencies produced their targets. GSA's lack of information on these methods limits its ability to oversee agencies' fleet optimization efforts and help agencies ensure that their fleets are the right size and composition to meet their missions cost-effectively.

In addition to data-related challenges, agency officials identified three broad fleet management challenges: meeting energy requirements, such as requirements for acquiring alternative fuel vehicles; uncertainty regarding the allocation of funding to fleet management activities; and ensuring that fleet managers have adequate expertise. Agencies have pursued or are pursuing a variety of strategies to address these challenges. These include the fleet optimization process, which calls for agencies to determine how best to fulfill requirements for alternative fuel vehicles; using a working capital fund, which provides a steady stream of funding; and providing online training for fleet managers.

_____ United States Government Accountability Office

Contents

Figures

Abbreviations

DHS	Department of Homeland Security
DOD	Department of Defense
DOE	Department of Energy
FAST	Federal Automotive Statistical Tool
FMIS	fleet management information system
GSA	General Services Administration
OGP	GSA's Office of Government-wide Policy
OMB	Office of Management and Budget
USDA	Department of Agriculture
VA	Department of Veterans Affairs

GAO U.S. GOVERNMENT ACCOUNTABILITY OFFICE

441 G St. N.W.
Washington, DC 20548

July 31, 2013

The Honorable Jeff Sessions
Ranking Member
Committee on the Budget
United States Senate

Dear Senator Sessions:

Federal agencies (excluding the U.S. Postal Service) spend about $3 billion annually to acquire, operate, and maintain about 450,000 civilian and non-tactical military vehicles, including passenger vehicles, trucks, and other vehicles such as ambulances and buses. Agencies can purchase these vehicles or lease them from the General Services Administration (GSA).[1] In recent years, Congress, the Office of Management and Budget (OMB), and the President have raised concerns about the size and cost of federal agencies' fleets. For example, in May 2011, the President issued a memorandum which, among other things, directed agencies to determine their optimal fleet inventories, using a methodology which emphasizes elimination of unnecessary vehicles and ensuring the cost-effectiveness of maintaining these inventories. In addition, recent legislative proposals have called for reductions in agencies' fleets.[2] Given these concerns, you asked us to review efforts to reduce federal vehicle fleet costs. This report addresses (1) the extent to which selected federal agencies use leading practices to manage their fleets, including the size and cost of their fleets, and (2) any challenges these agencies face in managing their fleets and strategies they use to address these challenges.

We assessed the extent to which the following agencies use leading practices to manage their fleets: the Departments of Agriculture (USDA), the Interior (Interior), Homeland Security (DHS), and Veterans Affairs (VA); and the United States Air Force (Air Force) and the United States Army Corps of Engineers (Army Corps) within the Department of Defense. Collectively, these agencies account for about 46 percent of the

---

[1] In certain instances, federal agencies may lease vehicles from commercial sources without prior approval or permission from GSA.

[2] See e.g., S. 417, 113th Cong. (2013).

roughly 450,000 civilian and non-tactical military vehicles maintained by the federal government (excluding the U.S. Postal Service).[3] In selecting these agencies for our review, we considered both civilian and military agencies with fleets of more than 5,000 vehicles. We looked for variation in fleet characteristics, such as age of passenger vehicles, changes in fleet size from 2005 to 2011, and changes in fleet composition (owned versus leased) from 2005 to 2011, with the goal of capturing a range of agency characteristics. Within USDA, Interior, DHS, and VA, we selected the subagencies with the largest fleets and selected a sufficient number to account for two-thirds of each department's non-tactical fleet. Consequently, in USDA we reviewed the Natural Resources Conservation Service and Forest Service; in DHS we reviewed U.S. Customs and Border Protection and Immigration and Customs Enforcement; in Interior we reviewed the National Park Service, Fish and Wildlife Service, and Bureau of Land Management; and in VA we reviewed the Veterans Health Administration. Within these four departments, we focused most of our work on these subagencies' management of their fleets, except in areas where the department level has primary responsibility, such as reporting to GSA on department-wide plans to determine and achieve optimal fleet inventories. Specifically, except where noted, we focused our work on fleet management practices, such as the collection and analysis of fleet cost data, of these eight subagencies as well as the Air Force and Army Corps. Throughout this report, we refer to these subagencies and their departments as well as to the Air Force and Army Corps as "agencies."

To determine the extent to which these selected federal agencies use leading practices to manage their fleets, including the size and cost of these fleets, we first identified key leading fleet management practices. To do so, we interviewed recognized fleet management experts from consulting companies and private, local government, and nonprofit entities as well as representatives of fleet management associations. To identify agency practices, we reviewed agency fleet management policies, procedures, plans, and other documentation on their fleet management practices and conducted interviews with fleet management officials at our selected agencies. We also obtained information from agencies on their fleet management information systems and on the types of data that they maintain in these systems and consider in making

---

[3]The U.S. Postal Service has about 213,000 vehicles.

GAO-13-659 Federal Vehicle Fleets

investment decisions, such as decisions about whether to own or lease vehicles. In addition, we examined selected agencies' assignments of home-to-work and executive vehicles. To select agencies for our review and to describe changes in selected agencies' fleet inventories over time, we used data in GSA's Federal Fleet report and additional data provided by the agencies. We assessed the reliability of this data by reviewing program documentation and quality assurance tests and discussing data elements with GSA and agency staff responsible for these data and found the data sufficiently reliable for these purposes. To identify any challenges these agencies face in managing their fleets and strategies they use to address these challenges, we interviewed agency fleet managers from our selected agencies. We also obtained the views of GSA officials and the experts identified above about these challenges and strategies. We analyzed these interviews to identify the challenges that agency fleet managers identified most frequently and strategies agencies are pursuing to address these challenges. Further details about our scope and methodology can be found in appendix I.

We conducted this performance audit from July 2012 to July 2013 in accordance with generally accepted government auditing standards. Those standards require that we plan and perform the audit to obtain sufficient, appropriate evidence to provide a reasonable basis for our findings and conclusions based on our audit objectives. We believe that the evidence obtained provides a reasonable basis for our findings and conclusions based on our audit objectives.

Background

The size and cost of federal vehicle fleets have been subjects of concern for many years.[4] In 2002, OMB sent a memorandum to the heads of executive branch agencies directing them to examine the size of their vehicle fleets and report the size, composition, and cost of their fleets as part of their budget submission process. In 2004, we reported that because of a lack of attention to key vehicle fleet management practices, the agencies we reviewed could not ensure their fleets were the right size

---

[4]We previously reported on changes in the sizes of selected agencies' fleets from fiscal years 2005 to 2011. See GAO, *Federal Fleets: Overall Increase in Number of Vehicles Masks that Some Agencies Decreased Their Fleets,* GAO-12-780 (Washington, D.C.: August 2, 2012.)

or composition to meet their missions.[5] Most recently, in May 2011, the President directed each federal agency to determine its optimal fleet inventory—including the number and types of vehicles needed—and to set targets for achieving this inventory by December 31, 2015. Key goals of this process are to eliminate unnecessary vehicles, ensure the cost-effectiveness of maintaining vehicle inventories, and meet alternative fuel vehicle goals.[6]

From fiscal years 2002 through 2012, the number of federal civilian and non-tactical military vehicles (excluding postal vehicles) increased 19 percent, from about 364,000 to 450,000 vehicles. Federal agencies use vehicles—specifically non-tactical vehicles such as passenger cars and trucks, and special purpose vehicles (e.g., ambulances and buses)—to carry out their missions. See table 1 for a breakdown of the fleets at the agencies we selected to study. Reported total costs associated with these agencies' fleets in fiscal year 2012 ranged from $48 million for the Army Corps' fleet of 8,041 vehicles to $523 million for DHS' fleet of 50,170 vehicles.

[5]GAO, *Federal Acquisition: Increased Attention to Vehicle Fleets Could Result in Savings,* GAO-04-664, (Washington, D.C.: May 25, 2004.)

[6]The memorandum directed that all new light duty vehicles leased or purchased by agencies as of December 31, 2015 be alternative fuel vehicles. Alternative fuel vehicles are vehicles that operate using an ethanol blended fuel, compressed natural gas, or batteries, among other fuels.

Table 1: Fleets at Selected Agencies, Fiscal Year 2012

Agency	Total number of vehicles	How agencies use these vehicles
DHS	50,170	DHS uses its vehicles across the United States to support its missions of preventing terrorism and enhancing security; securing and managing American borders; enforcing immigration laws; safeguarding and securing cyberspace, and ensuring resilience to disasters. **Vehicle types most commonly used:** light trucks, sedans, sport utility vehicles, and vans.
Customs and Border Protection	26,587	
Immigration and Customs Enforcement	13,580	
Interior	**33,975**	Interior operates its vehicles in rugged terrain and remote locations to support the department's mission of managing the nation's natural resources and cultural heritage; providing scientific and other information about those resources; and honoring trust responsibilities or special commitments to American Indians, Alaska Natives, and affiliated island communities. **Vehicle types most commonly used:** trucks, sport utility vehicles, and passenger sedans.
Bureau of Land Management	5,451	
Fish and Wildlife Service	7,195	
National Park Service	11,808	
USDA	**41,665**	USDA operates its vehicles in cities, rural communities, and National Forests across the United States and uses them to support the departments' varied missions, including food safety inspections, agricultural and forestry research, fire suppression, resource management, and law enforcement. **Vehicle types most commonly used:** trucks, sedans, sport utility vehicles, and vans.
Forest Service	20,235	
Natural Resources Conservation Service	9,516	
VA	**17,381**	VA uses vehicles to help provide health care, benefits, and memorial services to America's veterans and their families. The Veterans Health Administration uses most of these vehicles to assist in its mission of providing comprehensive care to more than 8.8 million veterans a year through its health care facilities, including 152 medical centers and nearly 1,400 community-based outpatient clinics. **Vehicle types most commonly used:** sedans, vans, and light trucks.
Veterans Health Administration	14,819	
Air Force	**47,384**	The Air Force vehicle fleet operates in various terrains supporting the following mission categories: aircraft platforms, civil engineering, base maintenance, first responders, force support, nuclear support, and tactical support. **Vehicle types most commonly used:** trucks, sedans, and vans.

Agency	Total number of vehicles	How agencies use these vehicles
Army Corps	8,041	The Army Corps fleet supports missions throughout the nation such as engineering, design and construction and real estate for the Armed Forces; water resources development and management; recreation; environmental cleanup and restoration; research and development, and disaster assistance. **Vehicle types most commonly used:** trucks, sedans, and vans.

Source: GAO analysis of information provided by agencies.

Federal agencies are responsible for acquiring, maintaining, and managing their vehicle fleets. They are responsible for deciding the number and type of vehicles they need and how to acquire them, including whether to own or lease them and when to replace them. Four of our selected agencies—USDA, Air Force, DHS, and Interior—own most of the vehicles in their fleets. VA and the Army Corps, lease most of the vehicles in their fleets. Agencies must develop a maintenance program for their owned and commercially leased vehicles. Further, agencies must operate their fleets in a manner that enables them to fulfill their mission and meet various federal requirements and directives that affect their fleets and fleet management. These include various statutes, executive orders, and policy initiatives that direct federal agencies to, among other things, collect and analyze data on the costs of operating their fleets, reduce petroleum consumption, acquire alternative fuel vehicles, and eliminate non-essential vehicles. (See table 2.) In addition, agencies must follow federal vehicle management regulations.

Table 2: Selected Statutes, Executive Orders, and Policy Initiatives Affecting Management of Federal Agencies' Fleets

Statute, executive order, or policy initiative	Year enacted or issued	Description
The Consolidated Omnibus Budget Reconciliation Act of 1985[a]	1986	Requires agencies to have a centralized system to collect and analyze data on the costs of their motor vehicle operations, including acquisition decisions, in order to improve the management and efficiency of their fleets and reduce costs.
Energy Policy Act of 1992[b]	1992	Requires that alternative fuel vehicles make up 75 percent of light duty vehicles acquired by federal agencies operating fleets of 20 or more vehicles in metropolitan statistical areas with populations of 250,000 or more.
Office of Management and Budget memo to federal agencies	2002	Requires agencies, as part of their budget submission, to report the size, composition, and cost of their fleets for the current year and to project costs for the next 3 fiscal years.
Executive Order 13423[c]	2007	Set goals in various energy efficiency areas and directs federal agencies to increase alternative fuel consumption by 159.4 percent (or 10 percent annually over the previous year) by 2015, from a 2005 baseline.

Statute, executive order, or policy initiative	Year enacted or issued	Description
Energy Independence and Security Act of 2007[d]	2007	Requires federal agencies to achieve at least a 20 percent reduction in annual petroleum consumption and a 10 percent increase in annual alternative fuel consumption by 2015 relative to a fiscal year 2005 baseline. Also prohibits federal agencies from acquiring any light duty motor vehicle or medium duty passenger vehicles that are not a low greenhouse gas emitting vehicle.
Executive Order 13514[e]	2009	In an effort to reduce greenhouse gas, the executive order directs federal agencies to reduce petroleum consumption by 30 percent or 2 percent annually by 2020, from a 2005 baseline.
Presidential Memorandum on Fleet Management	2011	Calls on federal agencies to lead the way in meeting the goal of reducing oil imports by, among other activities, determining the optimum size of their fleets and eliminating non-essential vehicles.

Source: GAO analysis of selected federal statutes, executive orders, and policy initiatives

[a]Pub. L. No. 99-272, § 15302, 100 Stat. 82 (Apr. 7, 1986).

[b]Pub. L. No. 102-486, § 303, 106 Stat. 2776 (Oct. 24, 1992).

[c]Strengthening Federal Environmental, Energy and Transportation Management, 72 Fed. Reg. 3919 (Jan. 26, 2007).

[d]Pub. L. No. 110-140, §§ 141, 142 (Dec. 19, 2007).

[e]Federal Leadership in Environmental Energy and Economic Performance, 74 Fed. Reg. 52117 (Oct. 8, 2009.)

GSA plays a key role in helping agencies manage their fleets. GSA's Office of Government-wide Policy (OGP) promulgates federal vehicle management regulations, issues guidance on federal fleet operations, and provides reports on the federal fleet. Federal regulations on fleet management include requirements regarding agencies' fleet management information systems, vehicle replacement policy, and vehicle fuel efficiency, among other things.[7] OGP also establishes policies and issues guidance to help agencies manage their fleets effectively and meet federal requirements. Guidance includes bulletins on various aspects of fleet management, including fleet management information systems and methodologies for determining the optimal fleet size for agency fleets. OGP also promotes interagency collaboration through various committees and councils, including the Federal Fleet Policy Council,[8] and has sponsored an annual conference on fleet management. GSA's OGP

[7]We previously reported that, while GSA promulgates regulations regarding the federal fleet, GSA officials indicated the agency lacks enforcement authority. See GAO-12-780.

[8]The Federal Fleet Policy Council provides a mechanism for coordinating federal vehicle management programs and policies, reviewing new technologies and automated systems, and analyzing the impact of current and proposed regulations, laws, Executive Orders, and international agreements. It is composed of representatives of federal agencies that operate federal motor vehicle fleets.

is also responsible for reviewing annually the Federal Automotive Statistical Tool (FAST) submissions from agencies. FAST is a web-based reporting tool, jointly sponsored by GSA and the Department of Energy (DOE), for agencies to report data on their fleets, such as number of vehicles, costs, and miles driven. FAST is used to satisfy statutory and regulatory reporting requirements and GSA uses it to produce an annual Federal Fleet Report.

GSA's Fleet and Automotive organization manages vehicle-purchasing and vehicle-leasing programs that offer federal agencies an array of automotive products, including alternative fuel vehicles, sedans, light trucks, buses, and heavy trucks. GSA purchases over 50,000 vehicles annually for federal agencies at prices that, according to GSA, are an average of 17 percent below the manufacturer's invoice price.[9] Supported by a network of regional Fleet Management Centers, GSA also leases more than 200,000 vehicles to over 75 federal agencies. Federal agencies may also lease from commercial vendors in certain instances.[10]

Selected Agencies Follow Leading Practices for Fleet Management to Varying Degrees

We identified three leading practices for fleet management: 1) maintaining a well-designed fleet management information system (FMIS), 2) analyzing life-cycle costs to inform investment decisions, and 3) optimizing fleet size and composition and found that the selected agencies in our review follow these practices to varying degrees. Most of the selected agencies lack the data needed to support sound fleet decision making and oversight and some of their fleet data systems are not integrated with other key agency systems. None of these agencies are fully analyzing lifecycle costs to make vehicle investment decisions. All of the agencies we examined have carried out an internal process for determining their optimal fleet size and composition and have set targets for achieving these optimal inventories, but most have not provided GSA, which reviews these targets, with clear information on the methods they used for producing them.

[9]The vehicle price to the agencies includes GSA's one percent surcharge to administer the purchase.

[10]According to GSA officials, an agency that lacks specific statutory authority to purchase or hire passenger motor vehicles as required by 31 U.S.C. § 1343(b), or has not been delegated leasing authority, is required to participate in the GSA centralized leasing program.

Leading Fleet Management Practices

We identified three leading practices for fleet management. We identified these leading practices based on views provided by fleet management experts in the private sector, local government, and fleet management associations.[11] We also compared these practices with legal requirements and GSA and OMB guidance related to federal fleet management. We found that these leading practices generally align with federal fleet management legal requirements and GSA and OMB recommendations, and, as discussed in the following sections, these recommendations identify specific actions that agencies should complete to adhere to these types of leading practices. In particular, GSA has issued guidance containing recommendations for following all of these leading practices. Finally, we obtained the views of GSA officials responsible for fleet management on these leading practices. Overall, according to the experts and GSA officials we interviewed, these practices provide a foundation for agencies to manage fleet costs while meeting their missions. They emphasized, in particular, that sound data systems provide the basis for the various types of analyses that are needed to make cost-effective investment decisions, such as decisions about whether to own or lease vehicles, and determine appropriate fleet size and composition. See table 3 for a fuller description of these leading practices.

Table 3: GAO Synthesis of Fleet Management Leading Practices

Practice	Description
Maintain a well-designed FMIS	An FMIS should include data from various parts of the organization on aspects of fleet management—such as inventory, costs, and utilization—and be integrated with agency financial and property management systems. Such a system allows managers to monitor performance and conduct analyses needed for management decision making.
Analyze life-cycle costs to inform investment decisions	Decisions about fleet investments should be informed by an analysis of the life-cycle costs of owning and operating a vehicle, such as acquisition, fuel, maintenance, and administrative costs. Such an analysis helps agencies make cost-effective decisions, including decisions about when to replace or dispose of an owned vehicle and whether to purchase or lease a new vehicle.
Optimize fleet size and composition	Determining the number of vehicles needed based on a consideration of certain factors, such as mission needs and vehicle utilization, that can provide a basis for downsizing fleets and reducing costs. Determining the proper mix of vehicles based on a similar analysis can also reduce costs.

Source: GAO analysis.

[11]We interviewed 9 experts, including representatives of two fleet management consulting companies, three public sector fleet managers, one private sector fleet manager, one fleet manager from a nonprofit and representatives of two fleet management professional associations. All noted the importance of maintaining a well-designed FMIS and conducting life cycle cost analyses and seven noted the importance of optimizing fleet size and composition. See appendix I for more information on our methodology.

Most Selected Agencies Lack the Data and System Integration Needed to Support Sound Fleet Decisionmaking and Oversight, but Improvement Efforts Are Under Way

Data Collection

All of the experts we interviewed noted the importance of maintaining an FMIS that tracks key data needed to manage the fleet. Additionally, GSA guidance states that a sound FMIS is needed for monitoring and analyzing fleet performance and meeting internal and external reporting requirements. The guidance recommends that agencies' FMISs capture a range of information and integrate with financial and property management systems to facilitate fleet analyses and reporting. Each of the selected agencies we studied had established an FMIS except for USDA's Natural Resources Conservation Service.[12]

Based on information provided by the selected agencies, most of their FMISs capture the majority of the types of fleet data recommended by GSA but none include all of these types of data. (See table 4.) GSA recommends that agencies' FMISs include data on fleet costs, vehicle acquisition, utilization, repair and servicing history, accidents, and disposal, among other things.[13] In some cases, agencies collect the recommended data but store some of it outside of their FMISs. Some of the data stored outside of the FMIS are kept in electronic systems, and in other cases, they are stored in paper file folders.

---

[12]Officials of the Natural Resources Conservation Service explained that the agency intends to transition to FedFMS, an FMIS developed by GSA to help agencies meet the requirement for a centralized fleet information system. This is expected to occur by the end of fiscal year 2013.

[13]GSA has reported that depending on their missions and structures, agencies may not need all of the recommended types of data in their FMISs, or may benefit from other data that is not explicitly recommended; however, agencies should have the data necessary to support relevant and comprehensive analyses.

Figure 1: Characteristics of Selected Agencies' Fleet Management Information Systems, 2013

Agency		Selected types of fleet data in FMIS[a]			
		Direct costs[b]	Indirect costs[c]	Utilization	Repairs and servicing history
DHS	Customs and Border Protection	◐	◐	●	●
	Immigration and Customs Enforcement	◐	○	◐	◐
Interior[d]	Bureau of Land Management	◐	◐	●	●
	Fish and Wildlife Service	●	◐	●	●
	National Park Service	●	◐	●	●
USDA	Forest Service	●	●	●	◐
	Natural Resources Conservation Service[e]	○	○	○	○
VA	Veterans Health Administration	◐	○	●	●
Air Force		◐	◐	●	●
Army Corps		◐	○	●	◐

● All data stored in FMIS and fleet cost data readily distinguishable from non-fleet cost data

◐ Some data stored in FMIS; or, fleet cost data not readily distinguishable from non-fleet cost data

○ No data stored in FMIS

Source: GAO analysis of questionnaires completed by these agencies and interviews with agency officials.

[a]GAO asked agencies to identify a single system as their FMIS and to report on what data are stored in that system. Fleet data are sometimes collected and stored in systems other than the FMIS, such as financial and property management systems. For information about whether an agency's FMIS is integrated with its financial and property management systems, see table 5.

[b]For the purposes of this review, direct costs include data on fleet costs associated with capitalized value, depreciation, all fuel, vehicle modifications, repair, and preventative maintenance, which are types of data recommended by GSA.

[c]For the purposes of this review, indirect costs include data on fleet costs associated with facilities, equipment, shop supplies, staffing costs, staffing training, and administrative costs, all of which are types of data recommended by GSA. To facilitate required analyses and reporting recommended by GSA, indirect fleet costs should be readily distinguishable from other indirect costs.

[d]Interior uses a single, centralized property management system as the department-wide FMIS.

[e]The Natural Resources Conservation Service does not currently have an FMIS.

The type of data missing most frequently from selected agencies' FMISs are data on costs associated with their fleets, especially indirect costs. According to GSA's recommendations, cost data should include direct expenses, such as fuel, repair, and vehicle depreciation, as well as indirect costs attributable to the fleet, such as expenditures associated with personnel.

Six of the nine agencies with FMISs that we reviewed reported to us that their FMISs do not capture all direct fleet costs. Most selected agencies keep at least some direct cost data in locations other than in an FMIS, such as in a financial management information system. For example, of the nine agencies with FMISs:

- five reported that they collect data on vehicle modification costs and accessory equipment, but some of the data are not stored in the FMIS; and

- three reported that they track some or all of their fuel costs outside of the FMIS.

In addition, three officials noted that some of their direct cost data lacked the detail needed to help them track life-cycle costs and make decisions such as when to replace vehicles.[14] For example, officials from DHS's Customs and Border Protection told us that certain details on maintenance and repair costs may not be reported due to the limitations of their current fleet payment card, making life-cycle cost analysis difficult to conduct.

With regard to indirect costs, eight of the nine agencies with FMISs that we reviewed reported to us that their FMISs do not capture all indirect fleet costs, or that the indirect costs cannot be readily discerned from other non-fleet costs. GSA defines indirect costs as any cost that cannot be ascribed to a particular vehicle or class of vehicles. Examples of indirect costs include most personnel costs, office supplies, building rental, and utility costs. While GSA identifies in its guidance the types of indirect costs that agencies should capture in their FMISs, it has not provided agencies with guidance on how to estimate those costs.[15] Indirect costs can be challenging to estimate because they may reflect the salaries of employees who only work on fleet management part-time

---

[14]Also, officials from Interior's Bureau of Land Management, Fish and Wildlife Service, and National Park Service told us that while maintenance and repair cost data are in Interior's FMIS, they do not know how to access this data and run reports on the life-cycle costs of specific vehicles because they are transitioning to a new system, the capabilities of which they are still learning.

[15]GSA officials told us that they provide a variety of resources to help agencies identify, but not estimate, indirect costs. For example, additional information on definitions of direct and indirect costs is available in GSA's FAST system.

or buildings that are only used partially for fleet-related purposes. Some agencies have not yet developed an approach for estimating these costs. For example, officials of Interior's Bureau of Land Management, and VA's Veteran's Health Administration told us that they lack a method to attribute a certain percentage of indirect costs, such as of facilities and equipment, to fleet management. In some cases, total personnel and facility costs are stored in the agencies' FMISs but the costs specifically associated with the agency's fleet are not readily distinguishable. For example, DHS's Customs and Border Protection's FMIS records data on facility costs, but it does not have the capability to separate facility costs associated with fleet management from total facility costs.[16] Out of the nine agencies with FMISs that we reviewed:

- eight reported that their FMIS does not include data on facility costs, or that facility costs in their FMIS are not readily attributable to fleet management;

- seven reported that their FMIS does not include data on staffing costs, or that staffing costs in their FMIS are not readily attributable to fleet management; and

- three reported that their FMIS does not include data on fleet-related equipment costs, including office and shop equipment, and tools.

Only one agency, USDA's Forest Service, reported that it captures all of the indirect fleet-related cost data recommended by GSA and can readily distinguish fleet costs from other indirect costs. For example, Forest Service officials track all fleet–related program management costs—such as personnel, facility, travel, and supply costs—and include them in the Forest Service's fleet costs. Forest Service officials explained that it is critical that the agency capture all fleet-related costs, because it charges the programs and functions that use the vehicles much like how GSA charges lessees.[17]

---

[16]Also, Interior officials who maintain the department's FMIS told us that it is capable of providing indirect fleet-related costs but that these costs would need to be determined though an accounting analysis of overall staffing and facility costs.

[17]Forest Service collects payment for the use of any vehicle. For example, a program is charged a monthly base rate plus a cost-per-mile charge when an employee of that program uses a specific vehicle.

In addition, of the nine agencies with FMISs we reviewed, one reported that it does not keep all of its data on vehicle utilization in its FMIS and three reported that they do not keep all their data on repairs and servicing in their FMIS.[18] Officials from DHS's Immigration and Customs Enforcement told us that fleet officials in headquarters have access to limited data on vehicle utilization because some utilization data are gathered by the mission groups that use the vehicles and are not shared with headquarters.[19] A few agencies also reported that limitations of the fleet payment cards they use to record transactions have impaired their ability to gather detailed data on servicing and repairs. Some cards record the cost of maintenance, but do not collect information on the type of maintenance performed.[20]

The lack of an FMIS with comprehensive data on fleet-related costs can make monitoring and analysis needed for fleet management challenging. For example, several agency officials said that gathering data on the type of maintenance performed on vehicles through methods such as reconciling receipts or using paper logs can make it difficult for fleet managers to perform timely analyses and guide fleet decisions. As explained in forthcoming sections, key analyses of agencies' fleets that are essential for sound investment decisions and management of fleet size and composition depend on complete and accurate data, particularly data on costs and utilization. Furthermore, the lack of complete data in agencies' FMISs can impair the validity of reporting on federal fleets, and could therefore impede the ability of GSA, OMB, and Congress to oversee the performance of these fleets. According to GSA officials, data gaps compromise the reporting of accurate agency fleet costs in the FAST system. In particular, because some agencies do not track all costs

---

[18]Furthermore, USDA's Natural Resources Conservation Service, which does not have an FMIS, maintains monthly usage logs which manually track plate number, trip date, origin, destination, and mileage.

[19]Immigrations and Customs Enforcement has three primary mission groups, each which has its own fleet manager and fleet staff. These three mission groups are responsible for the majority of the Immigration and Customs Enforcement vehicles. Officials in headquarters have access to utilization indicators such as mileage and fleet payment card activity, but do not have regular access to utilization data such as number of trips or number of passengers.

[20]Several fleet managers reported that switching to a different payment card can be challenging. Fleet managers may not have the authority to select a new card, changing cards may have contractual implications for other functions within the agency, and not all fleet payment cards are universally accepted by vendors.

associated with their owned or leased vehicles, the expenditures associated with all vehicles may appear lower than they actually are. GSA uses the data that agencies report to produce its annual Federal Fleet Report, which is used to report statistics such as costs per mile for owned and leased vehicles. However, because these reports may not fully reflect the costs of all vehicles, those statistics may be misleading, limiting the usefulness of this report for oversight of federal fleet costs.[21]

System Integration

Four agencies' FMISs are not integrated with financial or property management systems (see table 5). In other words, data cannot be passed from one system to another for processing and analysis. GSA recommends that agencies integrate their FMISs with financial and property management systems and GSA officials explained that this integration can improve data accuracy and completeness and reduce duplication of data entry.[22] Agency officials noted that integrating these systems can be challenging for various reasons, including legacy systems that use different data fields, competing internal data requirements, lack of authority over the systems to be integrated, and lack of funding for upgrades.[23] While there are many reasons that systems may not be integrated, this division of information can make it challenging to perform timely analyses of fleet costs and performance and to report on fleets. For example, the Army Corps keeps financial information in a system that is not integrated with their FMIS, which officials said causes duplication of data entry and makes annual reporting more difficult. Similarly, GSA officials reported that when systems are not integrated, users will enter data into the required reporting system of record, and may not have time

---

[21]According to GSA officials, the costs associated with GSA leased vehicles in this system are more accurate, because the leasing cost data that GSA provides to agencies, which they then roll up and input into the system, include all leasing costs. However, these costs do not include indirect fleet costs agencies incur when leasing from GSA. Vehicles leased from GSA comprised 30.2 percent of the federal fleet—including the United States Postal Service—in 2011.

[22]We have previously reported that integrated systems can promote efficiency. See *Information Technology: FDA Needs to Fully Implement Key Management Practices to Lessen Modernization Risks,* GAO-12-346 (Washington, D.C.: March 2012) and *Organizational Transformation: A Framework for Assessing and Improving Enterprise Architecture Management,* GAO-10-846G, (Washington D.C.: August 2010).

[23]The costs of an FMIS vary depending on the agency's needs. Air Force has invested approximately $6.2 million in its customized fleet management information system since 2006. GSA's FedFMS system is currently free to agencies, and will cost 15 cents per month, per vehicle, once GSA begins to charge for the service.

to repeat the data entry process for the FMIS. Lack of data greatly reduces the usefulness of FMISs to conduct fleet analysis.

Figure 2: Integration of Selected Agencies' Fleet-Management Information Systems with Financial and Property Systems, 2013

Agency		FMIS integrated with	
		Financial management system	Property management system
DHS	Customs and Border Protection	✓	X
	Immigration and Customs Enforcement[a]	X	✓
Interior	Bureau of Land Management	✓	✓
	Fish and Wildlife Service	✓	✓
	National Park Service	✓	✓
USDA	Forest Service	✓	✓
	Natural Resources Conservation Service[b]	N/A	N/A
VA	Veterans Health Administration	X	X
Air Force		✓	✓
Army Corps		X	X

✓ Systems are integrated

X Systems are not integrated

Source: GAO analysis of questionnaires completed by these agencies.

Note: Integration in this context means that data can be passed from one system to another, which can then process the data.

[a]The FMIS of DHS' s Immigration and Customs Enforcement contains some fleet financial data, including the capitalization and depreciation of assets.

[b]The Natural Resources Conservation Service does not currently have an FMIS.

Improvement Efforts

Some agencies we reviewed are making efforts to upgrade and automate their data collection, which could provide them with additional data recommended by GSA as well as additional detailed information to improve analysis and reporting. Most of the experts we interviewed noted the usefulness of automated data collection to provide timely and accurate information to guide fleet decisions.[24] In addition, if data are entered automatically, fewer personnel hours would be needed to collect, reconcile, and enter data. Several agencies are seeking to adopt fleet payment cards that will provide them with additional data on certain types of financial transactions, which would increase their data on direct fleet costs. For example, officials from USDA's Natural Resources Conservation Service told us that, in addition to implementing an FMIS, it will obtain vehicle and repair cost data from the new USDA fleet card program by the end of 2013.[25] Officials anticipate that the new fleet card will help them collect cost data that their previous card did not collect accurately or completely. Similarly, DHS's Immigration and Customs Enforcement is pursuing the capability of importing fuel and maintenance cost data from fleet payment cards. Four agencies are also exploring GPS systems that are capable of collecting data on utilization, greenhouse gas emissions, and direct costs such as scheduled maintenance and fuel consumption. For example, VA's Veterans Health Administration is pursuing efforts to use GPS based devices to upload data, including utilization and direct cost data, directly into its FMIS.

In 2012, GSA recommended that DHS, USDA, Interior, and VA obtain centralized, department-wide FMISs.[26] Various efforts are under way at these departments to address these recommendations, as well as efforts to integrate systems with property and financial management systems. (See table 6.) Interior currently possesses a centralized, department-wide FMIS, which its agencies are either using or plan to use soon. DHS, USDA, and VA do not currently possess such an FMIS, but are exploring new ways to store and share fleet data. For example, USDA is adopting FedFMS, an FMIS developed by GSA for federal agencies, for its

---

[24]Examples of automated data entry include fleet payment cards that capture detailed financial transaction data when purchases are made, technology such as scanners to automatically read vehicle identification numbers, and GPS.

[25]Fleet cards that capture detailed data can be a powerful tool, according to some experts we interviewed. These experts said that access to detailed data, such as fuel grades used or the precise parts that were repaired on a vehicle, allows fleet managers to more accurately analyze trends and better target their cost reduction efforts.

[26]As noted previously, the Consolidated Omnibus Budget Reconciliation Act of 1986 required federal agencies to have a centralized system to collect and analyze data on the costs of their motor vehicle operations. While all but one of the agencies that we reviewed within these four departments possesses an FMIS, these FMISs, with the exception of those used by Interior's agencies, are for the particular agency's use and are not part of centralized, department-wide systems.

agencies, with the exception of the Forest Service.[27] Also, VA plans to adopt a centralized FMIS and is examining various options for doing so. The Air Force and Army Corps already possess centralized FMISs and are pursuing additional interfaces between systems that will provide additional cost information.

Table 4: Fleet Management Information System Integration Improvements Under Way or Planned at DHS, Interior, USDA, VA, Air Force, and Army Corps

Agency	Improvements under way or planned
DHS	DHS is currently developing an asset management data warehouse that is expected to, among other things, compile fleet data and ultimately serve as the single source of record for all fleet inventory, acquisitions and operational information. This effort is expected to be complete by the end of fiscal year 2014.
Interior	Agencies within Interior are currently using—or are in the process of transitioning to— the department-wide FMIS. According to Interior, this FMIS is fully integrated with department financial and property systems. All of the agencies we reviewed are currently using this system, and the system is expected to be used department-wide by the end of calendar year 2013.
USDA	USDA is in the process of integrating data from its current property management system with FedFMS. USDA anticipates that FedFMS will capture all transactions and costs for owned and leased vehicles, except for those under Forest Service, which uses a separate FMIS. The new system is expected to be operational by the end of fiscal year 2013.
VA	VA reported that it has considered many systems, including FedFMS, but has yet to identify an FMIS that will meet all of its needs. VA is continuing to evaluate systems, and hopes to determine the best fit before the end of fiscal year 2013.
Air Force	By December 2014, Air Force plans to complete an interface between its FMIS and another internal system that contains some maintenance, repair, accident, direct cost and indirect cost data.
Army Corps	Army Corps is working with IT personnel, the Department of the Army and GSA to have multiple systems interfaced, including the FMIS, financial management system and the property system. This effort is expected to be complete by the end of fiscal year 2014.

Source: GAO presentation of information provided by agencies.

The steps these agencies are taking to improve their data collection and integration of their data systems have the potential to improve their ability to access and analyze data related to fleet management. However, these efforts are in various stages of completion and it is too early to tell whether they will fully address the problems we have identified. While agencies are making some progress, as previously discussed, some have not yet developed an approach for estimating indirect costs associated with fleet management. This is a particular problem when fleet

---

[27]According to USDA, the Forest Service has additional reporting requirements because of its working capital funding that FedFMS is unable to meet. However, Forest Service will continue to use its current FMIS and provide periodic reporting to the department.

management is assigned as a collateral duty and facilities are used for fleet management as well as other functions. GSA officials told us that they believe that a number of agencies have not developed such a method. As noted previously, GSA's current guidance on FMISs does not discuss how agencies can determine indirect costs. Providing additional guidance to agencies on a method to estimate indirect fleet costs for owned vehicles would be one step toward improving the overall quality of fleet data for agency decision making. As discussed in the next section, without complete fleet cost data, including indirect costs, agencies are unable to perform comprehensive analyses to determine the most cost-effective course of action, such as whether to lease or own vehicles. Also, as discussed previously, without complete cost data on their fleets, agencies' ability to accurately report on these costs is impaired.

Selected Agencies Are Not Fully Analyzing Life-Cycle Costs to Make Key Vehicle Investment Decisions

According to all fleet management experts we interviewed, life-cycle cost analysis, which captures vehicle costs from the beginning to the end of vehicle ownership, helps agencies make cost-effective fleet investment decisions, such as decisions about the best time to replace a vehicle they own. OMB requires agencies to analyze total costs to inform investment decisions.[28] Further, GSA's fleet management guidance recommends that agencies use life-cycle cost analysis to make vehicle replacement decisions and make decisions about whether to purchase or lease a vehicle. When agencies consider life-cycle cost information along with information on costs and benefits of alternatives or their effectiveness in meeting fleet objectives,[29] they can better evaluate investment alternatives and make choices that cost effectively meet their mission.

For example, the manager of the fleet of Troy, Michigan, an expert we consulted, told us that he used life-cycle cost data from Troy's fleet to show that the lifecycle of police vehicles can be extended without causing problematic downtime. Instead of replacing vehicles at the city's 60,000 mile recommendation, Troy's life-cycle cost analysis showed that police

---

[28]OMB Circular A-94 provides general guidance for conducting cost-effectiveness analyses, which should consider alternative means of meeting program objectives and comprehensive estimates of the expected benefits and costs to society. In addition, A-94 states that lease-purchase analyses should compare the net discounted present value of the life-cycle cost of leasing with the full costs of buying or constructing an identical asset.

[29]Fleet objectives include meeting environmental and socioeconomic goals (such as the number of alternative fuel vehicles needed) established in law, regulation, or policy.

vehicles did not need to be replaced until 90,000 miles. Conversely, the manager of the fleet of Portland, Oregon, another expert we consulted, told us that Portland used data on the life-cycle costs of vehicles by class to reduce patrol car ownership from 16 years to 5 years (or 100,000 miles) because this replacement cycle is what kept annual costs of vehicle ownership to a minimum.

Vehicle Replacement Analysis

Officials at two of the agencies we reviewed—Air Force and the National Park Service—reported that they incorporate elements of life-cycle cost analysis into their vehicle replacement decision-making process. Three fleet management experts we consulted noted that owned vehicles should be replaced around the time that their operating costs (mainly maintenance and repair costs) begin to outweigh their resale value. GSA's fleet management guidance says that an ideal fleet practice is for an organization to develop replacement guidelines based on empirical analysis of the relationship between cumulative usage and total vehicle ownership costs, such as depreciation[30] and maintenance and repair costs. Air Force fleet managers told us that they consider the previous 2 years of maintenance costs and depreciation figures to make vehicle replacement decisions. The National Park Service has developed an equipment (vehicle) replacement guide, but the vehicle replacement analyses that the agency provided did not depreciate the value of the vehicle over its life-cycle or consider increases in maintenance and repair costs as the vehicle ages.

The other agencies, we reviewed, however, acknowledged that they do not analyze life-cycle costs to make vehicle replacement decisions.[31] According to GSA officials, these agencies typically follow minimum federal vehicle replacement guidelines[32] (part of GSA regulations) or internal agency guidelines combined with professional judgment about when to replace vehicles. For example, officials of DHS's Immigration and Customs Enforcement told us that the agency generally follows minimum

---

[30]According to GSA, depreciation, or the decline in the value of a vehicle, should be counted as a cost each year as part of the cost of owning a vehicle.

[31]Army Corps and VA have fleets that are 90 percent and 75 percent leased, respectively, so, according to GSA and these agencies, they have less of a need to conduct vehicle replacement analysis since GSA conducts this analysis for leased vehicles for these agencies.

[32]41 C.F.R. § 102-34.270.

federal fleet replacement guidelines, but also analyzes each vehicle on a case-by-case basis. According to Immigration and Customs Enforcement officials, some vehicles may be doing well and kept longer, while others may have repair problems and may be disposed of. However, according to fleet management experts we consulted, without life-cycle cost analysis that uses an agency's own data, agencies will not have full information to make vehicle replacement decisions and may incur higher costs as a result. For example, if vehicles are kept past the point when their operating costs begin to outweigh their resale value, agencies may incur larger maintenance and repair costs as vehicles age and may require a larger fleet to accommodate vehicles that are undergoing repair work.

Lease versus Ownership Analysis

Eight of the 10 agencies that we reviewed told us that they are analyzing life-cycle costs to make lease versus ownership decisions, but our review of examples they provided indicates that some agencies do not consider all types of costs in their analysis. Some do not conduct this type of analysis at all. Fleet management experts and GSA have recommended that agencies base decisions about whether to purchase or lease vehicles on a comparison of the direct and indirect costs projected for the life-cycle of the owned vehicles to the total lease costs over an identical life-cycle.[33] The following bullets illustrate the range of lease versus ownership analyses that our selected agencies conducted:

- According to Forest Service officials, the Forest Service conducts a lease versus ownership analysis that includes a range of life-cycle costs. It has developed a structured "lease versus ownership" decision tool that, according to the officials, leads fleet managers to an informed decision about whether to own or lease a vehicle. Forest Service officials told us that direct and indirect costs are factored into the life-cycle cost analysis of any given vehicle because all costs have

---

[33]Some costs can be excluded if they are the same for the leasing and purchasing options. One agency and one fleet management expert commented that when making lease versus ownership decisions, it is important to include the cost of aftermarket equipment installation, like heavy duty bumpers, for law enforcement vehicles because this affects the breakeven point for lease versus owned decisions.

to be charged to its sub-agencies, including salaries and facilities, to make its vehicle fleet management system viable.[34]

- Six other agencies conduct lease versus ownership analyses, but these analyses sometimes do not include some key direct costs, such as depreciation, and indirect costs, such as costs associated with facilities, equipment, and staffing. For example, Interior's Fish and Wildlife Service and National Park Service provided us with a lease versus ownership analysis that included direct costs, such as depreciation and maintenance costs, but not indirect costs.

- Officials of USDA's Natural Resources Conservation Service and VA's Veterans Health Administration told us that they do not regularly conduct lease versus ownership analyses. Natural Resources Conservation Service officials told us that they lack the information system necessary to conduct this analysis regularly. Veterans Health Administration officials told us that some local fleet managers conduct lease versus ownership analysis, but most opt for leasing from GSA based on experience rather than a formal analysis.

Not considering a full set of costs or not conducting any lease versus ownership analysis may lead agencies to incorrectly conclude that one method of vehicle procurement is less expensive than another and could therefore lead to higher overall fleet management costs.

Agencies that do not conduct life-cycle cost analyses to make vehicle replacement or lease versus ownership decisions mainly cited problems related to their cost data and FMISs:

- As noted previously, most agencies we reviewed do not fully track data on costs in their FMISs. For example, officials at Interior's Bureau of Land Management and Fish and Wildlife Service told us that they lack detailed data on maintenance costs and the tools to collect this data for individual vehicles to make fully informed vehicle replacement decisions. Also, officials of VA's Veterans Health Administration and DHS' Customs and Border Protection told us that

---

[34]To fund vehicle replacement and operating expenses, USDA's Forest Service uses a working capital fund, which Forest Service programs reimburse for using fleet vehicles at rates representing the approximate cost to operate, maintain, and replace the vehicle. Rates are set to cover fixed costs such as depreciation and fleet program management.

they do not capture some indirect costs such as costs of staff, facilities, equipment, and data systems related to fleet management.

• Officials of USDA's Natural Resources Conservation Service told us that they cannot conduct a life-cycle cost analysis regularly because the agency does not currently have an FMIS. In addition, Interior officials told us that the National Park Service, Bureau of Land Management, and Fish and Wildlife Service are migrating to a new customized FMIS, the capabilities of which these agencies are still learning. According to Interior fleet management officials, implementation of a life-cycle cost analysis process within that system to make replacement decisions is at least a year away.

Improvement efforts under way in agencies' collection of data on fleet costs and in their FMISs, described previously, have the potential to improve their ability to capture and analyze life cycle costs. Officials from three agencies told us that they are seeking to improve their ability to perform life-cycle cost analyses through efforts to improve their data. For example, officials from Interior's Fish and Wildlife Service told us that past life-cycle cost analyses did not include depreciation or indirect costs, but they are working to develop this capability. Interior's Bureau of Land Management is undertaking efforts to improve its maintenance data to better enable life-cycle cost analysis. Officials from the Veterans Health Administration told us that improvement in depreciation and indirect cost data would help them conduct life-cycle cost analyses. They told us that they are implementing efforts to improve their FMIS to capture this data. While these various efforts may enhance agencies' abilities to determine costs associated with their fleets, as noted previously, some agencies lack a method for estimating indirect costs.

Agencies Have Reported to GSA Their Targets for Achieving Optimal Fleet Size and Composition, but GSA Lacks Information on the Basis for Targets

Most experts we spoke with told us that it is essential that fleet managers reduce the size of their fleet to the least amount of vehicles needed to meet the organization's mission. According to some experts, reducing fleet size holds great potential for cost savings. As noted previously, in a May 2011 memorandum, the President directed each federal agency to determine its optimal fleet inventory, including number and types of vehicles needed, using a methodology which emphasizes eliminating unnecessary vehicles and ensuring fleet vehicle composition is based on meeting agency missions. As directed by the memorandum, GSA subsequently issued guidance to agencies on a methodology to follow in determining their optimal fleet inventories.[35] The memorandum directed agencies to set targets for achieving this inventory by December 31, 2015, and to report their results to GSA by February 2012, along with their plans for achieving their 2015 fleet targets. GSA directed agencies, pursuant to the memo, to provide it with annual updates on progress toward meeting their optimal fleet size and composition targets.

DHS, Interior, USDA, VA, Air Force, and Army Corps carried out internal processes for determining their optimal fleet inventories, set targets for each fiscal year from 2012 through 2015 for achieving the optimal number and types of vehicles, and developed plans for achieving these targets. DHS, Interior, USDA, and VA provided department-level targets and plans.[36] These agencies reported their targets and plans to GSA in February 2012 and submitted updates in March 2013. While VA is planning to increase its fleet size by 8 percent from fiscal years 2011 to 2015 due to an increased demand for Veterans Health Administration services, the other agencies are planning reductions over this period ranging from 3 percent (Interior) to 15 percent (DHS). (See table 7.)

---

[35]General Services Administration, *GSA Bulletin FMR B-30 Motor Vehicle Management: Vehicle Allocation Methodology for Agency Fleets.* Washington, D.C.: 2011. This guidance updates previous guidance GSA issued in 2005 to federal agencies on developing and documenting a methodology for determining optimal fleet size and composition. See General Services Administration, *GSA Bulletin FMR B-9 Motor Vehicle Management: Documented Structured Vehicle Allocation Methodology for Agency Fleets.* Washington, D.C.: 2005.

[36]DHS, Interior, USDA, and VA noted in their plans that individual agencies within these departments had conducted their own studies. These departments then used these studies to develop department-wide targets and plans.

Table 5: Agency Actual and Planned Fleet Sizes, Fiscal Years 2011-2015, as of March 2013

Agency	2011 Actual Fleet Size	2012 Actual Fleet Size	2013 Planned Fleet Size	2014 Planned Fleet Size	2015 Planned Fleet Size	Projected percentage change in fleet size 2011-2015
DHS	56,534	50,170	49,596	49,036	48,307	-15
Interior	33,645	33,193	32,721	32,661	32,663	-3
USDA	43,399	41,665	40,846	40,545	40,340	-7
VA	16,421	17,381	17,398	17,668	17,694	8
Air Force	50,897	47,384	46,875	46,442	47,528	-7
Army Corps	8,634	8,041	8,084	8,057	8,097	-6

Source: GAO analysis of Federal Automotive Statistical Tool data.

All of the agencies, with the exception of VA, reduced their fleet sizes in fiscal year 2012. VA had planned to reduce its fleet by 45 vehicles to 15,174, but instead its fleet grew by nearly a thousand vehicles. VA explained that it is struggling to meet fleet size targets because of growing mission needs. Officials of the Veterans Health Administration, which is responsible for about 85 percent of VA's fleet, told us that their vehicles are generally used to transport disabled veterans to and from medical appointments and that their fleet has grown 49 percent since 2005 largely due to an increase in the number of service men and women needing their transportation services. They also noted that it is difficult to predict the agency's fleet needs up through 2015 because of the uncertainty of the number of veterans needing services, and the kinds of services needed.

While all of these agencies have set targets and developed plans for achieving their optimal fleet inventories by 2015 and most of them made progress in 2012 toward these targets, some may not be fully following GSA's recommended methodology for determining their optimal fleet inventories and therefore may be missing opportunities to ensure that their fleets are the right size and composition to meet their mission cost-effectively. The methodology recommended by GSA includes

- establishing specific vehicle utilization criteria to justify mission essential vehicles;

- conducting an assessment of vehicle utilization to determine how and the extent to which vehicles are used and apply the criteria to each vehicle;

GAO-13-659 Federal Vehicle Fleets

- identifying underutilized vehicles and determining the optimal number and type of vehicles needed in the fleet inventory by considering utilization, mission needs, and other alternatives such as public transportation; and

- reviewing and updating this type of study annually or sooner as mission needs change.

We found that nine of the agencies in our review have defined utilization criteria, but one—the Air Force—has not.[37, 38] These nine agencies, or their departments, have established these criteria in policies or procedures, generally by specifying minimum numbers of miles, days, or trips a vehicle should be used in a given timeframe to be considered adequately utilized. Air Force officials told us that they review the bottom 10 percent of vehicles in terms of utilization on a periodic basis; however, specific utilization criteria are not included in Air Force's fleet management policies. Also, while DHS has established department-wide utilization criteria, Immigration and Customs Enforcement officials told us that these criteria are not used to make replacement or disposal decisions at the mission-group level.[39]

Furthermore, we found that eight of the agencies in our review have policies or procedures calling for annual or more frequent assessments of vehicle utilization, but two do not. Interior's National Park Service, for example, has established procedures for annually studying utilization and for replacing, reassigning, or disposing vehicles based on that study. USDA's Forest Service conducts an annual utilization study, requiring units to report their plans for moving, selling, or reassigning underutilized

---

[37]We focused our review of utilization criteria and assessment policies and procedures on the following 10 agencies and subagencies: DHS's Customs and Border Protection and Immigration and Customs Enforcement; Interior's Bureau of Land Management, Fish and Wildlife Service, and National Park Service; USDA's Forest Service and Natural Resources Conservation Service; VA's Veterans Health Administration; the Air Force, and the Army Corps of Engineers.

[38]In a previous review of selected federal agencies, we found that these agencies had not established policies that contain clearly defined utilization criteria and were not routinely conducting periodic assessments of vehicle utilization. See *Federal Acquisition: Increased Attention to Vehicle Fleets Could Result in Savings* (GAO-04-664), May 25, 2004.

[39]These officials did note that fleet officials in headquarters analyze utilization before any new acquisition can proceed. At Immigration and Customs Enforcement, vehicles are acquired and managed with mission group funding allocations and, as noted previously, the agency has three primary mission groups.

vehicles. Two agencies—VA's Veterans Health Administration and the Air Force—have established procedures to review utilization more frequently and reassign or dispose of underutilized vehicles. However, the fleet management policies of DHS' Immigration and Customs Enforcement and Customs and Border Protection do not specify how often they should review utilization. Officials at Immigrations and Customs Enforcement told us that officials at the mission group level analyze utilization for vehicles they might replace, but that the agency does not otherwise review utilization on a regular basis.[40] DHS officials have told us that the agency is updating its procedures on fleet management to include requirements in GSA's methodology for determining an optimal fleet inventory, including utilization criteria and assessments.[41]

GSA reviewed agencies' plans and targets in 2012 and provided recommendations for changes in some agencies' fleet size and composition targets to further reduce fleet costs. GSA recommended that some agencies consider further reductions in the sizes of their fleets, increase alternative fueled vehicles, reduce expensive commercially leased vehicles,[42] and consider further use of vehicle sharing, rental vehicles, or public transportation.[43] GSA officials explained that they made these recommendations if they believed that an agency had not planned significant changes in its fleet inventory or its plans did not demonstrate that it had conducted a thorough analysis. However, GSA officials noted that they had limited information on which to base its 2012 recommendations because most agencies did not provide it with information on the methods they used to produce their fleet size and composition targets. Only two of the six agencies we reviewed (DHS and

---

[40]These officials did note that utilization is discussed at monthly meetings on fleet issues.

[41]According to DHS officials, DHS headquarters has conducted an annual department-wide survey of utilization in each of the past 2 years in response to the May 2011 Presidential memo and GSA's guidance.

[42]For these agencies, average costs for commercially-leased vehicles ranged from 60 percent higher than the average commercially-leased costs government-wide (VA) to over 400 percent higher than the government average (DHS).

[43]In its recommendations to agencies on reducing fleet size, GSA noted that, where it is not mission required, vehicles assigned to a single employee should be eliminated. Such vehicle assignments would include vehicles assigned to individuals on a home to work basis and vehicles assigned to agency executives. (See app. II for further information on our selected agencies' assignments of vehicles on a home to work basis and assignments of executive fleet vehicles.)

USDA) included a detailed description of these methods in the plans they submitted to GSA.[44] For example, DHS outlined step-by-step how it went about producing these targets, including, among other things, the data it captured, the department-wide utilization criteria it used, and how it assessed fleet utilization. However, in the 2012 plans they submitted, Air Force, Army Corps, Interior, and VA provided little or no information on the methodologies they used.

As of May 2013, GSA officials told us they were reviewing updated agency plans submitted in March 2013 and would provide further recommendations on agency targets and plans. The 2013 plans submitted by our selected agencies contain information on various topics related to fleet management, including the agency's FMIS and efforts to control fleet size and cost, but do not contain information on key aspects of the methods agencies followed in determining their optimal fleet inventories, such as how they identified underutilized vehicles using established criteria. According to GSA officials, it would be helpful for their review of agency plans and targets if they had information on how agencies conducted their analyses, including key aspects of their methods such as the utilization criteria they used, how they assessed utilization, and how they considered these and other factors in determining their optimal fleet inventories. The President's memorandum did not specify that agencies should provide this information to GSA and GSA has not requested this information. Reviews by external parties are a useful internal control activity and it is important that the external party gain a sufficient understanding of the agency's relevant operations and activities.[45] However, GSA plays an important role in providing guidance to federal agencies on managing their fleets effectively and, without information on methods agencies used to produce their optimal fleet size and composition targets, its ability to determine if the basis for agencies' targets is sound, if changes in these targets are appropriate, and if improvements in agencies' methods are needed is limited. Without such informed oversight, opportunities to fully identify changes in fleets that can reduce costs, based on appropriate methods, may be missed.

---

[44]DHS noted that a full analysis had not been done of all of its agencies' fleets, but that the department planned to complete a more comprehensive analysis in 2013.

[45]See GAO, *Internal Control Management and Evaluation Tool* (GAO-01-1008G), August 2001.

Selected Agencies Have Adopted Strategies to Mitigate Such Challenges as Competing Requirements, Funding Allocation, and Lack of Expertise

As previously discussed, data availability and integration of data systems are key challenges that affect many aspects of fleet management; however, agency officials also identified three additional, broad challenges: multiple and competing energy requirements, the allocation of funding to fleet management activities, and ensuring that fleet managers have adequate expertise in a decentralized environment. The extent to which each agency faces these challenges varies. Nevertheless, these were the most common challenges cited across the agencies we reviewed. Agencies have pursued or are pursuing a variety of strategies to address these challenges, which include the fleet optimization process, leveraging Department of Energy (DOE) tools, using a working capital fund, and providing online training, among other things.

Some Agencies Struggle to Meet Multiple and Competing Energy Requirements

Seven agencies we reviewed identified multiple and sometimes competing energy requirements as a challenge to effective fleet management. As described earlier, a defined set of energy requirements and goals governs the federal fleet through statutes, regulations, and executive orders. However, we have previously reported that these statutes and orders were enacted and issued in a piecemeal fashion and represent a fragmented rather than integrated approach to meeting key national goals.[46] We have also noted that, because of these numerous and sometimes conflicting requirements and directives, fleet managers often lack the flexibility and tools to meet various energy goals, such as reducing petroleum consumption, energy consumption and greenhouse gas emissions. For example, agencies may not acquire light-duty or medium duty motor vehicles that are not low-greenhouse gas emitting vehicles,[47] and the May 2011 Presidential memorandum directed that by December 2015, all new light duty vehicles purchased or leased by agencies must be alternative fuel vehicles.[48] However, VA has reported that most alternative fuel vehicles that meet their mission needs do not

---

[46]See *Federal Energy and Fleet Management: Plug-in Vehicles Offer Potential Benefits, but High Costs and Limited Information Could Hinder Integration into the Federal Fleet,* GAO-09-493 (Washington, D.C.: June 2009) and *Opportunities to Reduce Potential Duplication in Government Programs, Save Tax Dollars and Enhance Revenue,* 11-318SP, (Washington, D.C.: March 2011).

[47]Pub. L. No. 110-140, § 141.

[48]Examples of alternative fuels include electricity, E85 (a blend of up to 85 percent ethanol and petroleum), and compressed natural gas.

qualify as low-greenhouse gas vehicles, making it difficult to meet both mandates.[49]

Officials from four agencies also noted that it is challenging to meet energy requirements in a constrained budget environment because some of the requirements may result in additional costs. Agency officials explained that given their choices, they still acquire the most cost-efficient vehicle option as directed by OMB, but they are selecting from a more expensive inventory due to the environmental requirements. Also, while agencies must increase alternative fuel use, alternative fuels are not yet universally available[50] and ways to address this problem can require additional expenditures. Officials from several of our selected agencies explained that they have acquired some hybrids that can be used in areas that lack alternative fuel infrastructure; however, hybrids can be more expensive to acquire than traditional fuel vehicles or flex fuel vehicles that can operate on traditional fuel or E85 fuel.[51] Similarly, a few agency officials reported that the requirement to reduce petroleum is compromised when users must drive out of their way to find an alternative fueling station.

The 2011 Presidential memorandum directs agencies, where practicable, to develop alternative fueling infrastructure, but agencies differ on the extent to which they are willing and able to make this investment. DHS has stated that such construction is too costly and not appropriate for their needs. VA has constructed 45 E-85 fueling stations at medical centers across the country, at a cost of approximately $17 million, and plans additional investment. Officials from three agencies reported that commercial vendors are reluctant to install alternative fuel tanks when the return on investment is not promising. Two agency officials also said that

---

[49]We have previously reported on the same challenge. See GAO-09-493 and GAO-11-318SP.

[50]According to May 2013 data from the Department of Energy, more than 36 percent of publicly-available compressed natural gas stations are found in just two states—California and Oklahoma. Also, E-85 stations are relatively uncommon. We have recently reported that E85 suppliers are concentrated in a few regions in the country. See *United States Postal Service: Strategy Needed to Address Aging Delivery Fleet*, GAO-11-386 (Washington, D.C: May 2011).

[51]GSA officials also stated that hybrids are typically more expensive than traditional fuel vehicles and noted that GSA adds a surcharge to leases to cover any additional incremental costs.

accessing non-commercial fueling sites can pose unique, though not insurmountable, challenges. For example, according to a Forest Service official, accessing alternative fuel located on military installations can be hindered by security concerns and differing payment systems. Negotiations to resolve these concerns can require investments of personnel time and effort, which represents additional cost.

The fleet optimization process required by the May 2011 Presidential memo,[52] financial assistance from GSA, and tools provided to agencies by the DOE can help agencies balance competing requirements and determine the best approach for meeting these requirements while minimizing cost. A key goal of the fleet optimization process is to determine what fleet size and composition would best meet the agency's mission while also adhering to requirements for alternative fuel and fuel-efficient vehicles. To assist agencies with the costs associated with meeting energy requirements, GSA recently announced an initiative that would assist agencies in paying for the increased cost of hybrid vehicles. If agencies choose to consolidate their agency-owned vehicles into the GSA Fleet inventory, GSA will fund the total incremental cost to replace eligible vehicles with new, leased hybrid sedans. DOE also offers a variety of tools to help agencies. For example, the alternative fuel locator on DOE's website helps agencies determine what kinds of alternative fuels are available in a given area, and allows fleet managers to place alternative fuel vehicles in appropriate locations. In addition, the Army Corps and DHS have used a DOE tool to project which alternative fuel vehicles would be appropriate replacements for some of their current inventories. Some DOE tools can encourage collaboration, which reduces the burden of meeting requirements and advances mutual goals. For example, USDA plans to use DOE's interactive map of vehicles that were granted waivers to use non-alternative fuels to help identify partners interested in supporting commercial development of alternative fuel infrastructure.

---

[52]According to DOE, the Presidential memorandum does not reconcile conflicting requirements that federal fleets increase use of alternative fuels, reduce petroleum use, and reduce greenhouse gas emissions, but the memorandum does require activities that will help meet existing requirements.

| Funding Allocation Can Affect Fleet Cost-Effectiveness | Uncertainty regarding the allocation of funds for fleet management activities can make it difficult for fleet managers to operate their fleets cost-effectively. Several agency officials and fleet experts explained that predictable and reliable funding streams better support sound fleet management and planning. For example, several officials explained that when there are unforeseen reductions in acquisition funds that can be used to replace vehicles, fleet managers are more likely to keep vehicles that are older and therefore more prone to mechanical failure. As explained previously, several fleet management experts cautioned that keeping older vehicles can result in larger and more expensive fleets. Some noted that in such cases, more vehicles need to be available since the chance of breakdown is higher. |

In some cases, fleet funding is allocated only for certain activities and may not be used for options that managers consider to be more cost-effective. For example, fleet officials from VA's Veterans Health Administration and USDA's Natural Resources Conservation Service reported that funds are sometimes allocated specifically for leasing or specifically to purchase vehicles. Officials said that the required procurement type is not always the most cost-effective, but they have no choice but to spend the money as directed. In other cases, funds allocated for a specific purpose become depleted, even though additional investment could result in overall savings. For example, Air Force fleet officials reported that as of March 2013, there are approximately 210 underutilized vehicles, including specialized vehicles, which cannot be moved to locations where they are needed because funding to transport vehicles has been exhausted and additional funds have not yet been approved.[53] Officials said that transporting those underutilized vehicles at a cost of approximately $2 million would help the Air Force avoid $20 million in potential acquisition costs for new vehicles.

Fleet officials cited two strategies that address challenges associated with the allocation of funds for fleet management: (1) using a working capital

[53]Air Force fleet officials stated that they submitted an internal business case to receive additional funds for transporting these specific vehicles, which is under review. As of May 31, 2013, the funding had not yet been approved.

fund[54] and (2) developing clear, data- based analyses on the predicted outcomes of specific funding changes. A fleet management consultant, one of the experts we interviewed, told us that his company has previously recommended working capital funds to help agencies better manage the vehicle replacement cycle. Similarly, a county-level fleet manager we interviewed reported that without its working capital fund, the county might not be able to replace vehicles at the optimal time due to budget constraints.

USDA's Forest Service and Interior's Bureau of Land Management are the two agencies within the scope of this review that have a working capital fund. Officials from these agencies said that a steady stream of available capital helped them to replace vehicles on schedule and avoid a fleet that needed excessive maintenance.[55] In addition, in 2004 GSA recommended that agencies should operate their fleets using a revolving fund or similar mechanism that allows them to capture all vehicle costs and provides them with the means to replace their vehicles in a timely manner. However, an agency must have statutory authority to establish such a fund. Moreover, even among agencies that possess the legal authority to establish a working capital fund, other hurdles may exist. For example, officials from Interior's National Park Service stated that while having a working capital fund could be advantageous and Interior possesses the legal authority to establish such a fund in any of its

---

[54]Working capital funds, which are a form of a revolving fund, are accounts that may receive reimbursements and advances from other federal accounts. They generally do not receive appropriations directly. In addition, they may accept revenues collected from nonfederal sources for the sale of government products, such as the sale of vehicles. We have previously found that a working capital fund is recommended by fleet experts because it provides a stable and timely source of replacement funding. See *Federal Motor Vehicles: Private and State Practices Can Improve Fleet Management*, GGD-95-18 (Washington, D.C.: December 1994).

[55]In 2012, Forest Service collected approximately $171 million and distributed approximately $170 million through its working capital fund. The Bureau of Land Management collected approximately $63 million and distributed approximately $50 million.

agencies, start-up costs are a substantial barrier, as are issues related to fund administration.[56]

The Air Force has programmed mission needs at every installation into an algorithm that allows decision-makers to see the "ripple effects" of specific funding changes. Officials stated that although funding may still be cut, it is done strategically and with the lowest overall impact on mission performance or with full knowledge of the consequences. Similarly, DHS's Customs and Border Protection has drafted a strategic plan that considers costs, benefits and resource availability to achieve prioritized goals, and an accompanying implementation guide to measure progress. One expert we interviewed suggested that having data and analysis to demonstrate the specific outcomes of funding changes will help to ensure that decisions regarding cuts or re-allocation are made with full knowledge.

Having Fleet Management as a Collateral Duty Makes Developing Expertise More Difficult

Officials of four agencies also noted that ensuring that fleet managers consistently possess adequate expertise can be a challenge. The majority of agencies we examined reported that fleet management is a part-time task for some of their managers, which can make it difficult to develop fleet expertise. Officials from these agencies said that fleet managers can be responsible for various tasks beyond their fleet duties, such as property management. Officials from three agencies explained that in rural, remote locations it is not cost-effective to pay for a full-time fleet manager since the fleet is smaller than in more metropolitan areas.[57] They also cautioned that being part-time does not automatically indicate a lack of expertise in fleet management. However, some officials also agreed that when an employee only commits a portion of work hours to fleet management it can be more difficult to manage the fleet, and it can be challenging to consistently train a cadre of part-time workers located in

---

[56]We have conducted work that discusses key operating principles associated with working capital funds and has examined the uses of this funding approach in several agencies. See *Intergovernmental Revolving Funds: Commerce Departmental and Census Working Capital Funds Should Better Reflect Key Operating Principles*, GAO-12-56 (Washington, D.C.: November 2011) and *Intergovernmental Revolving Funds: NIST's Interagency Agreements and Workload Require Management Attention*, GAO-11-41 (Washington, D.C.: October 2010).

[57]Officials did not provide information regarding when a full-time fleet manager would become cost-effective.

remote areas. Officials from Interior's Fish and Wildlife Service, for example, said that the challenge of training numerous, part-time employees has become particularly evident as the agency tries to implement Interior's new FMIS. Similarly, officials from USDA's Forest Service reported that it is challenging to establish and maintain expertise in an environment where responsibilities are divided among multiple employees in different locations. Moreover, two agencies reported that it is challenging to retain the expertise already possessed. For example, Air Force officials explained that there is high demand for knowledgeable fleet managers in the private sector, and the challenges associated with deployment coupled with pay differences can make it hard to retain skilled fleet managers. Similarly, officials of DHS's Customs and Border Protection told us that some managers have moved on to another job after they were trained.

Agencies use varying approaches to enhance the expertise of their fleet managers.[58] Approaches differ even among agencies within the same department. For example, within DHS, Customs and Border Protection has a specific training program for fleet managers, while Immigration and Customs Enforcement provides fleet management training on an as-needed basis. Officials from each of these agencies expressed that they believed their training policies met their specific needs. Below are a few strategies that various agencies have pursued to address the challenge of developing consistent fleet management expertise:

- **Sending personnel to the annual GSA conference:** Officials from several agencies reported that the annual FedFleet conference hosted by GSA was a valuable tool for developing and maintaining expertise. Some found the conference useful for teaching core skills, and others said it provided updates on the latest practices to experienced managers.[59]

---

[58]We have not reviewed the efficacy of any of these training strategies, as such an evaluation was beyond the scope of this review. It is not known if these strategies meet the training needs of fleet managers, or if agencies should provide additional resources and training.

[59]In 2013, GSA renamed this conference FedForum. Due to sequestration and government-wide budget cuts, GSA determined that projected attendance was not sufficient to support the conference in 2013.

- **Online training and tools:** The Army Corps provides an online toolbox that contains information on fleet management requirements and internal processes. Similarly, Interior's Fish and Wildlife Service provides online fleet management training, and National Park Service has established an online fleet management portal that provides a variety of resources, including virtual training.

- **Communication and collaboration strategies to share specialized knowledge:** Officials from Interior's Fish and Wildlife Service reported that regional offices and the program management offices collaborate on decisions involving heavy fleet equipment because the program offices have expertise in that area.

- **Consolidation of fleet functions and expertise:** Air Force is in the process of transferring its fleet functions to one office.[60] Air Force officials explained that although the transfer is complex and multi-staged, the consolidation will allow for enhanced fleet management. USDA's Forest Service is also actively seeking ways to reduce the number of personnel with part-time fleet responsibilities. Forest Service officials explained that they recently conducted a study which indicated that fleet performance could be improved if they reduced fragmentation of personnel, and are currently deciding how to consolidate some fleet duties. In April 2013, USDA's Natural Resources Conservation Service began piloting a centralized, national fleet management team to consolidate fleet functions and expertise, and minimize collateral fleet management duties.

Conclusions

Understanding where agencies might improve fleet management practices can inform ways to achieve fleet savings across agencies and address recent concerns about the size and cost of the federal fleet. Specifically, fleets should be well managed to provide appropriate and reliable transportation at the least cost, while meeting agency missions and achieving petroleum and greenhouse gas reduction goals. Complete data and well-designed FMISs are essential for the management of federal fleets. Most of the agencies that we reviewed lack the complete fleet data, particularly cost data, and some lack the integrated fleet data

---

[60]The Air Force vehicle fleet is centrally managed at the Headquarters Air Staff level (Pentagon) by Air Force Element Vehicle and Equipment Management Support Office. Some functions, such as procurement, are still in the process of being transferred to this office.

systems that would facilitate the analyses, such as life-cycle cost analysis, necessary to support sound fleet decision making. The steps these agencies are taking to improve data collection and system integration have the potential to improve their ability to access and analyze data related to fleet management, including their ability to capture and analyze life cycle costs. We are not making a recommendation to these agencies because of the actions they are currently undertaking, although it is too soon to tell if these actions will successfully address the issues we have identified.

While these agencies are making some progress in improving their data systems, some have not yet developed an approach for estimating indirect costs that are attributable to fleet management. Calculating indirect costs—such as costs for staff, facilities, and equipment—can be a challenge for some agencies when only a portion of these costs is attributable to fleet management. Current GSA fleet management guidance does not include a methodology to calculate these indirect costs. While developing such a method would only be one part of an agency's overall efforts to improve agency cost data to inform investment decisions, it is a necessary step. By not fully tracking and analyzing total fleet costs, including such indirect costs, some agencies may not have full cost information with which to analyze life-cycle costs and make cost-effective investment decisions, such as decisions about whether to lease or purchase vehicles, and may not be able to fully monitor and report on fleet costs.

Determining the number and types of vehicles truly needed by agencies—based on a thorough analysis of vehicle utilization, mission needs, and alternatives—also holds the potential for cost savings. The agencies in this review have made progress in determining their optimal fleet inventories and have set targets and developed plans for achieving these optimal inventories. However, GSA's lack of information on the methods agencies used in producing their targets limits its ability to identify and recommend opportunities for improvement, which could perhaps lead to additional fleet cost savings.

Recommendations

To help improve fleet management, we recommend that the Administrator of GSA take the following two actions.

1. Develop and publish guidance for agencies on estimating indirect costs attributable to fleet management to help ensure that agencies have complete and accurate cost data.

2. Request that when agencies submit their annual updates on their fleet optimization targets, they provide GSA information and supporting documentation on the methods that they used to produce their targets.

Agency Comments

We provided a draft of this report to the Acting Administrator of GSA and to the Secretaries of Agriculture, Defense, Homeland Security, Interior, and Veterans Affairs for review and comment. In commenting on this draft, GSA noted that it agreed with our findings and recommendations and that it intends to carry out the recommendations. DHS and the Department of Defense provided comments that included additional information on efforts they are taking to improve fleet management, especially systems for maintaining fleet data. GSA's, DOD's, and DHS's comments are reprinted in appendices III, IV, and V, respectively. In addition, DHS, USDA, and VA provided technical comments, which we incorporated as appropriate. Interior did not have any comments on this report.

We are sending copies of this report to interested congressional committees; the Secretaries of Agriculture, Defense, Homeland Security, Interior, and Veterans Affairs; and the Administrator of GSA. In addition, this report will be available at no charge on GAO's website at http://www.gao.gov.

If you or your staff have any questions about this report, please contact me at (202)512-2834 or Flemings@gao.gov. Contact points for our Office of Congressional Relations and Public Affairs may be found on the last page of this report. GAO staff who made major contributions to this report are listed in appendix VI.

Sincerely yours,

Susan Fleming
Director, Physical Infrastructure Issues

Appendix I: Scope and Methodology

We assessed the extent to which the following agencies use leading practices to manage their fleets, including the size and costs of these fleets: the Departments of Agriculture (USDA), Interior (Interior), Homeland Security (DHS), and Veterans Affairs (VA), and the United States Air Force (Air Force) and the United States Army Corps of Engineers (Army Corps) within the Department of Defense. Collectively, these agencies account for about 46 percent of the roughly 450,000 civilian and non-tactical military vehicles maintained by the federal government (excluding the U.S. Postal Service). When selecting these agencies, we considered both military and civilian agencies with fleets of more than 5,000 vehicles. We looked for variation in fleet characteristics, including: age of passenger vehicles, change in fleet size from 2005-2011, and change in fleet composition (owned versus leased) from 2005-2011, to ensure that we selected agencies with a range of fleet characteristics. We eliminated agencies that had been the subject of a fleet-related audit within the past 2 years,[1] with the exception of agencies covered in a recent report that stemmed from the same Congressional request as this review.[2] We considered those agencies to provide continuity of information. To select agencies for our review and to describe changes in selected agencies' fleet inventories over time, we relied on data in GSA's Federal Fleet report and on additional data provided by the agencies. We assessed the reliability of this data by reviewing program documentation and quality assurance tests and discussing data elements with GSA and agency staff responsible for these data and found the data sufficiently reliable for these purposes.

Within USDA, Interior, DHS, and VA, we selected the subagencies with the largest fleets and selected a sufficient number of subagencies to account for at least two-thirds of each agency's non-tactical fleet. Consequently, in USDA we reviewed the Natural Resources Conservation Service and Forest Service; in DHS we reviewed U.S. Customs and Border Protection and Immigration and Customs Enforcement; in Interior we reviewed the National Park Service, Fish and Wildlife Service, and Bureau of Land Management; and in VA we

---

[1]This included both GAO reports and reviews conducted by agencies' respective Inspector Generals. For example, we excluded the U.S. Postal Service because of a recent GAO report on their fleet. See *Strategy Needed to Address Aging Delivery Fleet*, GAO-11-386 (Washington, D.C: May 2011).

[2]See *Federal Fleets: Overall Increases in the Number of Vehicles Masks That Some Agencies Decreased their Fleets*, GAO-12-780. (Washington, D.C.: Aug 2012).

reviewed the Veterans Health Administration. Within these four departments, we focused most of our work on these subagencies' management of their fleets, except in areas where the department level has primary responsibility, such as in reporting to GSA on department-wide optimal fleet inventories. Specifically, except where noted, we focused our work on fleet management practices, such as the collection and analysis of fleet cost data, of these eight subagencies as well as the Air Force and Army Corps. Throughout this report, we refer to these subagencies and their departments as well as to the Air Force and Army Corps as "agencies."

To identify leading fleet management practices, we interviewed recognized fleet management experts from consulting companies and private, local government, and nonprofit entities as well as representatives of fleet management associations. We identified fleet management experts by determining if they met more than one of the following criteria: (1) winner of a fleet management award such as those sponsored by the American Public Works Association, (2) spoke at or organized a relevant fleet management conference such as GSA's FedFleet conference or the Government Fleet Expo and Conference, (3) served as a previous GAO expert, and (4) recommended by other fleet management experts. We interviewed 9 experts, including 2 representatives of fleet management consulting companies, 3 public sector fleet managers, one private sector fleet manager, one fleet manager from a nonprofit, and representatives of 2 fleet management professional associations. These experts include:

Consulting Companies

- Accenture

- Mercury Associates

Private, Public, and Nonprofit Fleet Managers

- Two fleet managers for cities with approximately 3,000 and 500 vehicles and pieces of equipment respectively (Portland, Oregon and Troy, Michigan)

- One fleet manager for a County with 1,800 vehicles (Hillsborough County, Florida)

- One private sector fleet manager overseeing more than 4,000 vehicles

- One fleet manager for a nonprofit overseeing more than 12,000 vehicles

Professional Organizations

- Automotive Fleet and Leasing Association

- National Association of Fleet Administrators

We compared practices these experts identified to legal requirements and GSA and Office of Management and Budget guidance related to fleet management. We also obtained the views of GSA officials on these leading practices. Based on the frequency with which practices were identified, as well as our professional judgment, we synthesized this information into a set of leading practices against which we compared agency practices. These leading practices are: (1) maintaining a well-designed fleet management information system, (2) analyzing life-cycle costs to inform investment decisions, and (3) optimizing fleet size and composition.

To determine the extent to which the selected federal agencies use leading practices to manage their fleets, including the size and cost of these fleets, we reviewed agency fleet management policies, procedures, plans, and other documentation on their fleet management practices and conducted interviews with fleet management officials at these agencies. We also developed a structured questionnaire sent to each agency regarding whether or not they have a fleet management information system (FMIS), the types of data that are maintained in their FMIS, whether their FMIS is integrated with property and financial management systems, and the efforts under way or planned to improve system integration and fleet data collection. We used the questionnaire responses, as well as supporting information gathered during interviews, to determine if an agency maintained an FMIS and if so, whether it stored all, some or none of the data elements recommended by GSA in that system. We used the information provided by agencies, such as the process that agencies follow in making decisions about whether to own or lease vehicles, to determine if agencies analyze total life cycle costs for their investment decisions. We also used information provided by agencies to determine how agencies are optimizing their fleet size and composition. As part of our review of fleet size and composition, we examined agencies' assignments of home-to-work vehicles and large or non-alternative fuel executive vehicles. These assignments are discussed in appendix II.

To identify challenges these agencies face in managing their fleets and strategies they use to address these challenges, we interviewed agency fleet managers from our selected agencies. We also obtained the views of GSA officials and fleet experts about these challenges and strategies. We analyzed these interviews to identify the challenges that agency fleet managers identified the most often and the strategies most frequently identified to address these challenges.

We conducted this performance audit from July 2012 to July 2013, in accordance with generally accepted government auditing standards. Those standards require that we plan and perform the audit to obtain sufficient, appropriate evidence to provide a reasonable basis for our findings and conclusions based on our audit objectives. We believe that the evidence obtained provides a reasonable basis for our findings and conclusions based on our audit objectives.

Appendix II: Home-to-Work and Executive Vehicle Assignments of Selected Federal Agencies

The agencies we covered all have procedures in place to determine, on a case-by-case basis, whether the assignment of home-to-work vehicles is justified based on mission. Of these agencies, DHS's Customs and Border Protection and Immigration and Customs Enforcement and Interior's National Park Service have the largest number of home-to-work vehicles. (See table below.) These vehicles are generally assigned for purposes of law enforcement duties and field work, such as patrolling the U.S. border and conducting and performing immigration law enforcement activities and field-level audit work. Agencies we reviewed have home-to-work policies in place at the department level, or have established policies at the agency or regional/local level establishing permissible uses of home to work vehicle assignments. For example, the National Park Service property management handbook states that all home-to-work vehicle assignments must be authorized by the Secretary of the Interior, and that monitoring of the use of home-to-work vehicles be monitored at the local level so long as an authorization is in effect. DHS home to work policy also requires a log be maintained to ensure use is for official purposes only, that a detailed analysis of proposed costs associated with home-to-work use be provided, and that these vehicles assignments be certified annually to the DHS Office of the Chief Administrative Officer.

The President's May 2011 memorandum to federal agencies on their fleet management directed, among other things, that agencies post on their respective websites the number of vehicles assigned to agency executives that are larger than a mid-size sedan or do not use alternative fuel.[1] Of the agencies we reviewed, DHS's Customs and Border Protection and Immigration and Customs Enforcement and USDA's Natural Resources Conservation Service have the largest number of such vehicles: 49, 20, and 20, respectively. In 2012, GSA noted that DHS as a whole retains a very large executive fleet of 90 luxury sedans and large sport utility vehicles and recommended a reduction in the size of this fleet and in the size of the assigned vehicles. In response, DHS stated that when their executive vehicles are up for replacement, they will closely examine the need for each, and, if still needed for mission purposes, it

---

[1]GSA subsequently issued guidance to agencies regarding fulfilling these requirements. See General Services Administration, *GSA Bulletin FMR B-32 Motor Vehicle Management: Posting Executive Fleet Vehicles on Agency Websites*. Washington, D.C.: 2011.

would consider replacing them with smaller, more fuel-efficient vehicles.[2] Other agencies we reviewed maintain smaller fleets of such executive vehicles that are either large or not alternative fuel vehicles, ranging from zero to 14.

Table 6: Home-to-Work and Executive Vehicle Assignments for Selected Agencies, 2013

Agency	Home-to-work vehicles	Home-to-work vehicle uses	Executive vehicles[b]
DHS			
Customs and Border Protection	1635	Canine operations, marine vessel transport, and law enforcement activities	49
Immigration and Customs Enforcement	8276	Law enforcement and field work	20
Interior			
Bureau of Land Management	270	Law enforcement and wildland fire response	0
Fish and Wildlife Service	426	Law enforcement	0
National Park Service	1,164	Law enforcement	0
USDA			
Forest Service	800[a]	Primarily law enforcement, also seasonal wildland fire response, and field work	0
Natural Resources Conservation Service	1	Economical for the government and employee	20
VA			
Veterans Health Administration	0	N/A	1
Air Force	2	Secretary of Air Force and Chief of Staff only	14
Army Corps	0	N/A	0

Source: Information provided by agencies and on agency websites.

Note: We did not assess the reliability of these numbers because they were not material to our findings, conclusions, and recommendations. [a]Estimate provided by agency.

[b]These numbers represent executive fleet vehicles that are larger than midsize sedans or are not alternative fuel vehicles.

---

[2]Also, DHS has noted that due to the unique nature of the U.S. Secret Service missions such as dignitary protection, exemptions are granted for them to acquire larger vehicles on an as needed basis.

Appendix III: Comments from the General Services Administration

The Administrator

July 15, 2013

The Honorable Gene L. Dodaro
Comptroller General of the United States
U.S. Government Accountability Office
Washington, DC 20548

Dear Mr. Dodaro:

The U.S. General Services Administration (GSA) appreciates the opportunity to review and provide comment on the draft report, "FEDERAL VEHICLE FLEETS: Adopting Leading Practices Could Improve Fleet Management" (GAO-13-659).

GSA agrees with GAO's findings and concurs with the recommendations below:

1. Develop and publish guidance for agencies on estimating indirect costs attributable to fleet management to help ensure that agencies have complete and accurate cost data; and
2. Request that agencies provide to GSA, when submitting their annual updates on their fleet optimization targets and plans, information and supporting documentation on the methods they used to produce their targets.

GSA, through its Office of Government-wide Policy, will develop and publish guidance for agencies on estimating indirect fleet costs. This guidance should help agencies achieve a complete and accurate picture of their indirect costs, such as salaries of personnel with fleet related duties. In addition, GSA concurs with and will adopt the recommendation for agencies to provide supporting documentation on their methods for determining their optimal fleet inventories to GSA as part of their annual updates.

Should you have any additional questions or concerns, please do not hesitate to contact me or Ms. Lisa Austin, Associate Administrator, Office of Congressional and Intergovernmental Affairs, at (202) 208-1806.

Sincerely,

Dan Tangherlini
Administrator

cc:
Susan Fleming, Director,
Physical Infrastructure, U.S. Government Accountability Office

U.S. General Services Administration
1800 F Street, NW
Washington, DC 20405
Telephone: (202) 501-0800
Fax: (202) 219-1243

Appendix IV: Comments from the Department of Defense

OFFICE OF THE UNDER SECRETARY OF DEFENSE
3000 DEFENSE PENTAGON
WASHINGTON, DC 20301-3000

ACQUISITION,
TECHNOLOGY
AND LOGISTICS

JUL 17 2013

Ms. Janet A. St. Laurent
Director, Defense Capabilities and Management
U.S. Government Accountability Office
441 G Street, N.W.
Washington, DC 20548

Dear Ms. St. Laurent:

This is the Department of Defense (DoD) response to the GAO Draft Report, GAO-13-659, "FEDERAL VEHICLE FLEETS: Adopting Leading Practices Could Improve Fleet Management," dated June 21, 2013, (GAO Code 541098). Detailed comments on the report recommendations are enclosed.

Sincerely,

Nancy L. Spruill
Director
Acquisition Resources and Analysis

Enclosure:
As stated

GAO Draft Report Dated June 21, 2013
GAO-13-659 (GAO CODE 541098)

"FEDERAL VEHICLE FLEETS: ADOPTING LEADING PRACTIVES COULD
IMPROVE FLEET MANAGEMENT,"

DEPARTMENT OF DEFENSE COMMENTS
TO THE GAO RECOMMENDATION

RECOMMENDATION: Request that agencies provide to GSA, when submitting their annual
updates on their fleet optimization targets and plans, information and supporting documentation
on the methods they used to produce their targets.

DoD RESPONSE: Concur. The Department acknowledges that improvements can be made in
how our non-tactical fleet is managed. In an aggressive effort to meet Executive, Federal and
Departmental regulations and to provide the Department of Energy (DOE), Office of
Management and Budget (OMB) and General Services Administration (GSA) accurate and
timely Fleet Management Information, the Department of Defense (DoD) has:

- appointed a Fleet Manager within the Office of the Secretary of Defense for
  Acquisition, Technology and Logistics for vehicle management oversight;
- rewritten non-tactical fleet management policy; and
- reengineered its asset management system and made it available to all DoD agencies,
  to fulfill all the fleet information and accountability requirements.

The Defense Property Accountability System (DPAS) has the capability to capture all
fleet data (including direct and indirect costs for life-cycle cost analysis) that will permit total
Fleet visibility within one system regardless of acquisition source (Lease/Owned); has seamless
integration between Fleet, Property and Financial management systems; will interface with
Federal Automatice Statistical Tool (FAST) for Data Call submissions; and contain Dispatch
functionality allowing real-time utilization visibility and recording to the Fleet Manager for
proper rotation and management of pooled vehicles. This functionality will enable frequent and
accurate utilization assessments to properly determine optimal fleet size and composition.

The only Fleet data currently residing outside of DPAS is the cost and utilization
information captured by GSA for DoD leased vehicles. The Department is working with GSA to
develop a seamless, electronic interface with those key GSA systems that house this essential
Fleet information into DPAS during FY14 so that we have the complete cost profile for our non-
tactical fleet. We agree that the lack of complete data is hampering our ability to make informed
fleet decision but believe the policy and management tools we are implementing will lead to
enhanced fleet management and simplified reporting.

2

Appendix V: Comments from the Department of Homeland Security

U.S. Department of Homeland Security
Washington, DC 20528

July 15, 2013

Susan A. Fleming
Director, Physical Infrastructure Issues
U.S. Government Accountability Office
441 G Street, NW
Washington, DC 20548

Re: Draft Report GAO-13-659, "FEDERAL VEHICLE FLEETS: Adopting Leading
       Practices Could Improve Fleet Management"

Dear Ms. Fleming:

Thank you for the opportunity to review and comment on this draft report. The U.S. Department
of Homeland Security (DHS) appreciates the U.S. Government Accountability Office's (GAO's)
work in planning and conducting its review and issuing this report.

DHS appreciates GAO's acknowledgement of the challenges agencies face in managing their
vehicle fleets to meet multiple and competing energy mandates while achieving mission
objectives. In this regard, DHS is currently working to enhance data availability and integrity
through development of a data warehouse that is expected to serve as the single source of record
for all fleet inventory, acquisitions, and operational information and to help facilitate decision
making. This effort is expected to be completed by the end of Fiscal Year 2014. DHS continues
to grow and mature, in part, by strengthening and building upon existing capabilities and
increasing efficiencies within its five key mission areas: (1) preventing terrorism and enhancing
security, (2) securing and managing our borders, (3) enforcing and administering our
immigration laws, (4) safeguarding and securing cyberspace, and (5) ensuring resilience to
disasters. An appropriately sized and managed vehicle fleet is critical to these efforts.

Again, thank you for the opportunity to review and comment on this draft report. Technical
comments were previously provided under separate cover. Please feel free to contact me if you
have any questions. We look forward to working with you in the future.

Sincerely,

Jim H. Crumpacker
Director
Departmental GAO-OIG Liaison Office

Appendix VI: GAO Contacts and Staff Acknowledgments

GAO Contact	Susan A. Fleming, 202-512-2834.
Staff Acknowledgments	In addition to the contact above, Judy Guilliams-Tapia (Assistant Director), Maria Edelstein, Kieran McCarthy, Alison Hoenk, Steve Rabinowitz, Russell Burnett, Tim Guinane, Josh Ormond, Crystal Wesco, and Colin Fallon made key contributions to this report.